SURVIVING COLLEGE
While Raising a Toddler

An inside look of unexpected happenings

nikki dillard
blueprint of an overkomer

Cover design by Femi N. Anderson
Manuscript Layout by Bummi N. Anderson

Copyright © 2013 Nikki Dillard. This book or parts thereof may not be reproduced in any form, stored in a retrieval system, or transmitted in any form by any means- electronic, mechanical, photocopy, recording, or otherwise- without prior written permission of the publisher, except as provided by United States of America copyright law.

ISBN-10: 0615901794

ISBN-13: 978-0615901794

TABLE OF CONTENTS

Dedication... pg. 5

Foreword…..………………………..…… pg. 7

Introduction……..…………………………….. pg. 9

Chapter One: Expect the Unexpected……….....…. pg. 11

Chapter Two: Stepping Stones ……………….. pg. 25

Chapter Three: Building a Support System………. pg. 36

Chapter Four: Faith in God ……………….……. pg. 46

Chapter Five: Toddlers' View .... pg. 52

Chapter Six: Making Time…….................. pg. 59

Chapter Seven: Climbing over the Mountain .... pg. 66

Poem: Don't Quit…....…..................... pg. 76

Acknowledgements ....…...... pg. 77

References…............................... pg. 79

*Christine,
you're greater
is coming!!!
Never give up, no matter what!*

DEDICATION

To this guy: Cayden. I wouldn't be who I am today if you were not in my life.

To my bff: thank you for being a listening ear when I needed to cry, vent, fuss, and whine and so much more! I love you much and so grateful to call you my friend!

FOREWORD

Life has a way of preparing one for things that they expect as well as the unexpected. Challenges have a way of shaping and molding one's character and give one the ability to persevere and move forward.

This is when Nakoasha Dillard comes to mind -- I can remember the very first time that I met Nakoasha; it was December 8, 2011 at First United Methodist Church located in Albany, Georgia. On that night I served as the keynote speaker -- for the Strive2Thrive Fall 2011 Graduating Class. Nakoasha was the emcee, and as she manned the platform, she spoke with poise and displayed a witty sense of humor, as her smile then and today brightens any room.

I further learned that Nakoasha was an active participant in the Strive2Thrive Initiative as a Circle Leader, one who takes the lead in their sphere of influence (or Circle) and make deliberant and intentional steps to become self-sufficient.

This book "Surviving College While Raising a Toddler" will stretch beyond the borders of Albany, Georgia. Single parents throughout the nation will be able to relate and embrace Nakoasha's story as they read and are enlightened on her journey, her struggle, and her triumph.

As you delve into the chapters of this book, you will see an incline of gradual steps that left behind tangible results in Nakoasha and Cayden's life. Her sacrifice for her son cannot be weighed on any scale, although you can count the number of her degrees, you cannot count her determination or drive. My mantra is simple "inside of every obstacle, there's an opportunity".

Nakoasha Dillard's obstacles have manifested into great opportunities that will continue to lay the foundation of her life. Look out!!! – For the best is yet to come!!!

Warmest Regards,

Vincent Alston

Friend

INTRODUCTION

Life as we know it. What exactly does it mean? Can we find the answers written in the "Policies and Procedures of Life" Manual? Is a there a "10 Steps to Surviving Life" self-help book written somewhere? I don't think that there is any one correct answer, remark, opinion, or statement that another human being can give that will provide true meaning to someone's life. The real answer lies within you, the person. I believe it is a daily learning process that continues until you leave this thing called life.

- N. Dillard

CHAPTER ONE: EXPECT THE UNEXPECTED

How do you take on the responsibility of another human when you are not even prepared to take care of yourself?

The choices that we make every minute determine what our life will be like. We can't control the unexpected loss of a loved one, tragic accident, unexpected job closing, etc., but we can make the informed and thoughtful decisions so that our life won't be as bad as we think it is now. One must be wary that any decision made can affect his/her life in a variety of ways.

SO MY STORY BEGANS……….

Imagine moving out of town to pursue your college degree only to find out after you have moved and gotten settled that you're carrying a little human being. Yep, this was me. You can only imagine the questions that ran through my head! I had transferred from Darton College in August 2008 and moved to Kennesaw, Georgia to attend Kennesaw State University (KSU) located about thirty minutes north of Atlanta. I could only think about all of the things I wanted to accomplish in life. I had it all planned out: I was going to pursue my Bachelor's in Biotechnology, obtain my Master's in some unknown major that I hadn't even decided at the time, and obtain my PhD in Biological Sciences. Prior to me moving, I spoke with the coach at KSU about my desire to play college basketball. After my college days, I was going to have a career in research for some big company, marry a tall, handsome, dark-skinned "smart-as-me" guy and live in this nice five bedroom, three bath, two garage split level house, that included an entertainment room and mini gym on the bottom level. Yep, those were my plans. But this major turning point in my life happened.

So here I am this 22-year old, basketball playing, always-on-the-go, Albany-born-and-raised young adult in the big city of Kennesaw, pregnant with family and friends being miles away. My oldest brother and his family lived one hour away from the school. I played in my mind over and over again - how could I ask him for help? My middle brother lived all the way in south Florida near Miami– so what help could he be to me? My youngest brother was… well I don't know what he was doing at the time but of course he couldn't help out.

My best friend who I had been friends with since freshman year in high school (and still counting today), was actually the first to know I was pregnant through a phone conversation. I told him I hadn't been feeling well the past few weeks but I figured it was because I was working double shifts at Red Lobster to earn extra money for the move to Kennesaw. His first words were a question of "You pregnant"? I told him I didn't think so and that I was just tired and worn out. He asked me had I seen my monthly, and as I sat and thought about it, I hadn't. He encouraged me to get a test just to "be on the safe side". I took his advice and told him I would call him back. It seemed like only mere seconds had passed and I was already calling him back with the results. As soon as he answered I said one word: YES. He didn't have any useful words of encouragement for me but said the typical thing a guy could say at this very life changing moment: "Aww man, so what you gonna do"? Fortunately for him he was on the other side of the phone so I could not jump through the phone and scream, "I don't know!!!" Didn't he know that already?

As I sat in the bathroom holding the "stick", no wild emotions emerged from me. I didn't cry or feel bad. I wasn't confused or hurt. I didn't pinch myself to see if I were sleeping or dreaming. I just sat there feeling numb. After sitting for what felt like an eternity (in real time... about fifteen minutes), I got up and went into the room. I was living with my brother and his family until school started and pondered how was I going to break the news to him and his wife. How would I tell my mom? I flopped on the bed and stared at the ceiling. It appeared that all my plans and dreams were floating out window. Although it wasn't the end of the world, I knew all my goals and dreams were about to be put on hold.

I made an appointment with my OB-GYN back home in Albany to confirm the news I had just learned. Unfortunately my doctor wasn't in town so on top of this new reality- I had to share this news with a doctor whom I've never seen. It wasn't until after I had gotten the "real results" from a medical professional that my emotions began to surface. It was confirmed and yes I was definitely pregnant. I was already five weeks! That did it. The tears ran down my face as reality set in. I was about to carry this person for nine months and then after that, attempt to raise him (as I found out later at my four month doctor visit that it was a boy). After my appointment, I went to my mom's house to gather the rest of my belongings. I had already enrolled in my classes so I decided to stay in Kennesaw for the semester. Driving to my mom's house, I didn't know what I was going to do. I just knew she would notice the fact that I was pregnant. Moms know and see everything! This particular weekend I went home, the conversation with her seemed to consist of how proud she was of me. This made me feel smaller than a mustard seed. She was talking about how I wasn't part of society's statistics (a young African American female with multiple children not doing anything for myself), and how I was going to school and working two jobs and on and on she went. Of course after she put me on this high pedestal, there was no way I could tell her this news that wasn't so great. I mean I am her only daughter and I wasn't even married and now I have a child on the way. I left that weekend with even more thoughts in my head.

On the way back to my brother's house, I called my cousin whom I looked to as a sister and told her the news. She was on my side and stated that if I needed anything that she would be there. Then she asked if I had told my mom and of course I hadn't gotten enough nerve to even mention my pregnancy. She said I had to do it so why not now? So I sat in the truck and called my mom. I told her I had something to tell her and I took what felt like a thirty minute pause and just spilled it. "Mom, I'm pregnant". Her reaction was definitely not what I expected: "Oh well you're on your own" and she hung up.

I bawled. I called my cousin back and cried like it was no tomorrow. I was expecting her to fuss or yell or something. But for her to say those words hurt deeper than anything. My cousin told me that I shouldn't cry and worry because my mom was in shock and that she would come around. She also said that I should not put too much stress on myself or the baby because I had a long drive ahead. So, I gathered myself and took the longest drive ever back to Kennesaw, Georgia.

Back at my brother's, I couldn't keep this secret. I was searching for a way to tell them when the opportunity presented itself. His wife and I were sitting on the back deck talking. She asked me was I excited about starting school and how would I manage away from home. I answered the questions briefly and then paused. "Well, I won't get to enjoy it much…I'm pregnant".

"What?" she whispered loudly. "Have you told your brother?"

Ha! Was that a serious question? None of my brothers knew this news and to tell my oldest one of all people was hard in itself. She didn't make it any better when she called him outside to join us and just stared at me to break the news. I took a deep breath and spilled it. "I'm pregnant". Now I don't remember what he said after that, but I do remember him running through his house holding his head yelling "Oh no! What are we to do?"

Now that had me laughing. That was the first laugh I had since I found out I was pregnant. Maybe it was because I didn't get the reaction I thought I would get, or maybe it was because he knew how I was feeling about the whole situation: unsure. The three of us sat at the kitchen table and discussed the "Ok she's pregnant, what's next" talk. He asked had I talked to mom and I told him what happened. My phone rang at that particular moment and it was her: MY MOM. I didn't answer. Well I couldn't answer, not after her reaction. So he talked to her for me. Afterwards he told me she said that she was just surprised and didn't expect that kind of news. She wanted to know if I was coming back home. The idea of me going back home was the last thing on my mind. I wanted to finish my plans...my goals...my dreams! But I had to think realistically. My brother and his wife opened up their home to me and my unborn child. His wife stated that she would be willing to keep the baby during the day while I was at school so that I could finish my degree. That sounded like a good plan except for the one hour commute to school every day. What would I do about a job? I knew I had to move back home with my mom and although I appreciated the offer my brother gave me, I didn't want to impose. After discussing what I should do, I decided to finish that one semester at Kennesaw State University and return home.

That semester at KSU was very hard. For the first couple weeks I contemplated what I should do about my pregnancy. I had thoughts of keeping the child and tried to figure out how my life would be if I did. The baby's father and I were not together, so I knew I had to raise the child as a single parent. There was the thought of aborting the baby, but because of the Christian home I was raised in, I knew it was wrong, and that thought was immediately dismissed. Then, I thought about carrying this baby for nine months and give it up for adoption, but what would that gain? Give a child up who had nothing to do with the wrong choice I had made just to continue my educational goals and to hang out and have fun? No. So I decided what I knew was best: bring the baby into this world and raise him.

This was my first trimester and I didn't know I would be feeling so many different hormonal and mood swings. I wrote my mom this long letter telling her about carrying the baby for nine months, how sorry I was, and how I felt I had disappointed her. My mom helped me through the semester by giving me encouraging words and keeping me motivated about school. I completed my first and only semester at Kennesaw then returned home.

CHAPTER TWO: STEPPING STONES

I have this new little person….now what?

Upon returning back home, I enrolled back into Darton College as I only had four classes to graduate with my Associate's degree. I was due to have my child on March 22nd.

On March 23, 2009, I was walking the hall in between classes at Darton College talking with a friend, and I felt a trickle down my leg. I rushed to the bathroom, but it was a false alarm. I told my friend I was going home to change because I had another class, but before I could even make it to my car a flood of water came rushing down my legs. My water had broken on campus! I called my mom and it seemed as if she got there in three seconds. I went into the hospital at 11:30 am and at 8:24 pm weighing 7 pounds 9 ounces and measuring 21 inches: Cayden Tristan Dillard had finally arrived! Thankfully I had no complications while in labor and out came this healthy boy.

All I could do was stare at this live human being who I had just given birth to. What happens now? How do I know when to feed him, when to change him, how to burp him? Then when he gets older, how do I know what to tell him about what's right and what's wrong when I am still trying to find my way? What about the girls and the "birds and the bees" talk? Whoa! One day at a time. I knew I needed my mom's help. She was and still is my main help and has been here for me since day one: literally.

Many young people think that raising a child is easy because all you have to do is change their diapers, feed them, and change their clothes. If that was the case, this country would be full of little ones walking around. Children are work. If it's all about self, then having a child is not for you. It takes a lot of sacrifice to raise a child. One must factor in that if the child gets sick, you have to be up in the middle of the night with him or her. You have to take off from work or school to go get them if something was to occur during the day. If you like to go out to party and hang with your friends, then keep it that way and delay having a child. All dreams and goals must be put on hold. The little person comes first. I'm not saying that the plans you have for your life must completely halt; they just cannot be achieved at the moment.

I could not just stay home and take care of my child. I had to provide for him because no one else would. He was my little person, a part of me. I also refused to be included into society's statistics. So I went out and did things that would help Cayden and me. I went to the local health department where they provide WIC (Women, Infants, and Children), a program that:

...provides nutrition education and supplemental foods to low income families. Participants receive a nutrition assessment, health screening, medical history, body measurements (weight and height), hemoglobin check, nutrition education, breastfeeding support, referrals to other health and social services, and vouchers for healthy foods.

I also knew I needed to get some health insurance for him so I went to the Dougherty County Department of Family and Children Services (DFCS) office and applied for Medicaid. I applied for food stamps as well to help with other nutritious food items that WIC didn't cover.

YOU MAY BE ELIGIBLE FOR FOOD STAMPS/MEDICAID BENEFITS IF:

…you are a citizen of the United States or have a certain legal alien status…you provide all of the required documents as proof of the household's situation… you and/or other household members comply with work requirements the household's monthly income does not exceed the income limits based on the number of people who live in the household…

Yes, I must admit I was ashamed at first to go there and apply because I am not the type to ask for help. Someone once told me "Use the services while they are being offered because you won't be on them forever".

Each and every day I am shooting towards my goal to be completely off of the system because it is designed to keep you on it. I will discuss the "system" later on in Chapter 7.

I knew that education was the key to getting Cayden and me to the next level. But first, I had to enroll Cayden into a daycare. How would I find a good one? How would I be able to leave him and know that he will be ok? To start searching for a good daycare, I began asking around. Word of mouth is the best form of communication when needing to get insight about things such as which companies are hiring, where the location of great dining areas and the best schools are, and where to look when searching for a home. Also word of mouth is useful when looking for a doctor to choose when one has a specific ailment. In my case, I needed the 411 on where to leave my child during the day so that I could make our life better.

I asked different people I knew and finally I settled on a church daycare. But wait! How was I going to pay for this daycare that charged $85+ per week? I found out the local Department of Family and Children Services (DFCS) also offered help to families needing childcare.

...Subsidized child care in Georgia is provided through the Childcare and Parent Services (CAPS) program to help low income families afford quality child care. The CAPS program is administered in all 159 Georgia counties through the county Department of Family and Children Services....

But in order to obtain this service I had to get a job. I found a job as waitress at Logan's Roadhouse. I was approved for childcare and my daycare fee was now $22 per week which was a great blessing!

I must admit that I don't remember too much of Cayden's early months because I was working long hours at Logan's Roadhouse. I even worked double shifts when my mom was able to keep Cayden during the evening. You would think this was enough to sustain us but it wasn't. In Georgia, most waitresses' hourly pay is $2.13/hour. That is why tipping is so important. The money waitresses make is what they have to live off of. I had to go to other resources for monetary help. Diapers, formula, bottles, clothes, etc. are all things needed to help in raising a child and they are expensive! Because the child's father and I were not together I knew I had to seek help. I went back to the local DFCS office and applied for child support.

Today's generational thinking about child support is not rational. The money obtained from this resource is to be used solely for the child. Not for clubs, parties, hairstyles and the up keep of the mother, but for the child's needs. My mom had to also explain to me that taking out child support was not a way to punish the father, but it was my right and his duty. She also said that anything pertaining to the child (housing, car, utilities, daycare, clothes, food…) the child support is to be used for. I had a better understanding of getting this support now.

Cayden's father and I were (and still are) on good terms, so I personally was not "out to get him" as I have heard is the case for other single moms.

I wanted to do everything in my power to make sure Cayden had everything he needed so I knew my journey had only begun. I wanted to continue to my education on a higher level, but first I needed a support system.

CHAPTER THREE: BUILDING A SUPPORT SYSTEM

It's not just a support system, but your life system

I knew that I could not walk this new journey alone and I needed help from somewhere, but where? The answer was not too far over the hill: MY FAMILY. Family is the one that will stick by your side through your most tough times. Thankfully, I have that kind of family. Although for my mom, her daughter being pregnant may have been unexpected at the time, Cayden had come so there was no turning back. This was her third grandchild but this is the one that she is able to be with every day.

I was living at home with my mom so she helped me whenever I needed it. When she had to return back to work, my aunt came over and sat with me. My aunt also, if my mom was not available, took me to my doctor and WIC appointments when needed. My loving grandmother cooked for me and boy was I ever happy! This type of support and love was what I needed and the thought of having a child out of wedlock didn't matter anymore.

Without the needed support of family and persons of close relation, a female raising a child alone has to endure the happiness, frustrations, hardships, brick walls and much more that comes with parenthood ALONE. There would be no mental, physical, and moral support. Spiritual guidance would not be there as well. The lack of support can bring on something known as Postpartum Depression. According to PubMed Health:

…postpartum depression is moderate to severe depression in a woman after she has given birth. It may occur soon after delivery or up to a year later. Most of the time, it occurs within the first 3 months after delivery.

Symptoms include and are not limited to: agitation or irritability, changes in appetite, feeling withdrawn or unconnected, thoughts of death or suicide, and trouble sleeping. A mother with postpartum depression may also: be unable to care for her or her baby, be afraid to be alone with her baby, have negative feelings toward the baby or even think about harming the baby, worry intensely about the baby, or have little interest in the baby. Although these feelings are scary, they are almost never acted on. One experiencing such feelings and thoughts should tell their doctor about them immediately.

The risk of Postpartum Depression is higher in women who are under the age of 20, currently abuse alcohol, take illegal substances, smoke, have a poor relationship with significant other or are single, and have little support from family, friends, and/or spouse or partner. Medication and professional talk therapy can often successfully reduce or eliminate symptoms. Having good social support from family, friends, and coworkers may help reduce the seriousness of postpartum depression, but may not prevent it.

Thankfully I did not suffer from Postpartum Depression but it was not and still isn't an easy journey that I'm travelling on. There have been many late nights up with Cayden wondering why he wanted to sleep throughout the day and then wake up every 2 hours through the night because he was hungry, needed changing, had gas or was just crying.

I remember this one particular night where I had to literally walk for 4 straight hours to get him to sleep. At the time, I was breastfeeding him and taking iron pills. That was good and bad. Good because I was getting my iron, bad because he was getting too much iron and it was causing him not to have a bowel movement. My mom would not let me give him any milk because he was gassy but nothing coming out. I knew my baby was hungry and I could only give him water until I could reach the doctor the next morning. It was 12:00 a.m. and whenever I tried to lay him down he would scream like I was hurting him. So I rocked him, patted his back, rubbed his tummy, talked to him, everything. He still would not go to sleep. He would close his eyes for a few moments and whenever I stopped doing the different techniques I thought would help him fall asleep, he popped his little eyes open. Finally I got up and walked him. I walked and rocked. And rocked and walked. I did this for 4 hours. In this middle of this, I sat down on the couch and held him with his head in my hands and his face towards mine. I said to him "Cayden mommy is very tired. Can you please just go to sleep"? I felt myself nodding off while holding him but thankfully I didn't drop him. I'm not sure how long I had nodded off, but when I opened my eyes, he was sleep. Whew! What a night. It was then and there that I knew I didn't want any more children, not if I had to do this alone! I don't even think he was 2 months when I decided this!

That is just one of the many incidents I remember directly. Next would come finding the right formula for him, getting the right pediatrician, getting his shots, making sure I remembered his doctor appointments, the potty training trial, him becoming more independent, the temper tantrums, and more. Yet, I cannot be Genie and blink and it all goes away. This little one is with me forever. Now that's something to think about! But although I had all this going on, I knew I still had to get my degree. I had the support system; I just needed to go for it.

As mentioned earlier, I had enrolled back into Darton when I returned home from Kennesaw in the spring semester of 2009. Because of the support and motivation of my family and friends, I was able to complete my classes and graduate May 2009 with an Associate of Science in Biomedical Technology. My ultimate goal was to return back to Kennesaw State and complete my Bachelor's but was unable to because of finances.

I did not want to attend Albany State University (ASU) at the time, so I enrolled at Albany Technical College (ATC) for the fall quarter in 2009. Enrolling into a technical school was different because while in high school, I was always told it was for students wanting to pick up a trade (welding, automotive, cosmetology, etc.) and I was pushed to go to a college or university because I was on the

College Prep level. But I wanted to do something different and after seeing all the different careers ATC offered I decided to attend. I wanted to take up Medical Assistanting but the program was closed. I had no other true interest and finally decided to do Pharmacy Technology; after all it was still in the health and science field and that was my career objective. I am glad I decided upon Pharmacy. I enjoyed the hands on experience in the class and while on internship. And my professor was great. She was like a mom to the students and was very understanding.

While in the program, they extended it from not only being able to obtain a diploma but one could take a few extra classes and receive their

Associate of Applied Science. So on September 2011, I graduated from Albany Technical College with both my diploma and Associate's in Pharmacy Technology. I was able to receive both because I had satisfied all requirements.

Graduating with a second degree was great and all, but what happens when you have the resources, the education, the mental, physical and emotional help, but you still feel like that's not enough to get you through certain circumstances?

CHAPTER FOUR: FAITH IN GOD
Depending on your spirituality for strength

Having the support of family and friends is great, but there are many times where I have had to turn to God and ask for his strength to help me make it through a single day. It can become very overwhelming in trying to juggle a toddler, work, school, church, and all the other extra activities I was involved in. There were days where it seemed like the light at the end of the tunnel had dimmed, but I had to remember that God was (and still is) telling me to seek out and live by Proverbs 3:5-6:

…Trust in the Lord with all thine heart; and lean not unto thy own understanding. In all thy ways acknowledge him and he shall direct thy paths.

I grew up in the church and I learned that God knows what best for you, and that He will never put more on me than I can bear. Yes the road may have seemed to get narrower the higher I travelled, but if I continued to trust and believe that he was by my side, I am and will be okay. This takes me back to one of my favorite poems:

God will never leave you nor forsake you. He is always there even when we can't seem to feel him.

FOOTPRINTS IN THE SAND

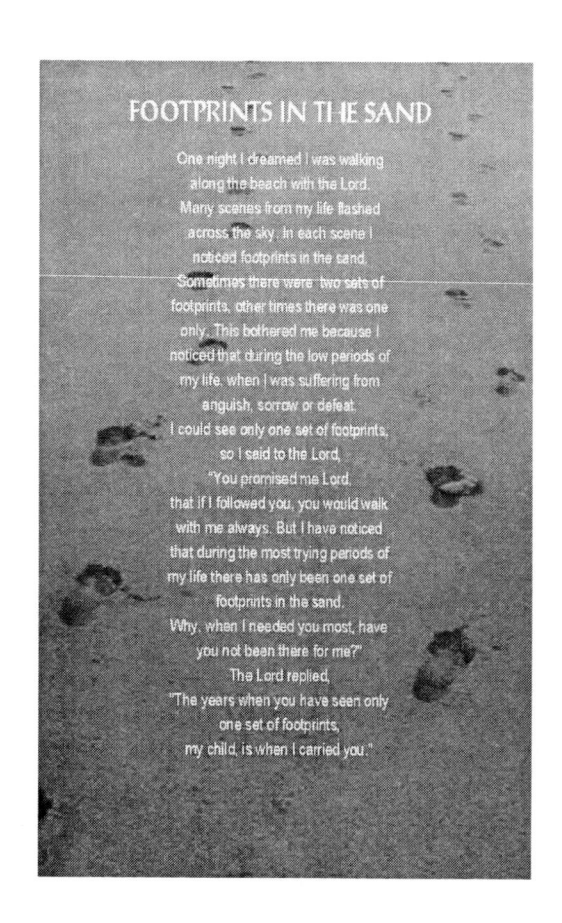

One night I dreamed I was walking along the beach with the Lord. Many scenes from my life flashed across the sky. In each scene I noticed footprints in the sand. Sometimes there were two sets of footprints, other times there was one only. This bothered me because I noticed that during the low periods of my life, when I was suffering from anguish, sorrow or defeat, I could see only one set of footprints; so I said to the Lord, "You promised me Lord, that if I followed you, you would walk with me always. But I have noticed that during the most trying periods of my life there has only been one set of footprints in the sand. Why, when I needed you most, have you not been there for me?" The Lord replied, "The years when you have seen only one set of footprints, my child, is when I carried you."

Attending church provided me with mental support and encouragement. I have learned that many young adults do not attend church because of the outward appearance the people in church portray. It seems as if a young person "messes up" or do not uphold the "law of the church" then they are frowned upon by the congregation; the very people who are supposed to be the backbone for the needy, a hand to the weak.

I once experienced something that was told to me by someone of the church and it left a feeling inside of me of uneasiness. Of course it had to do with me having a child out of wedlock. Now, I had already had this battle in my head about being pregnant, but then to have it readdressed to me from someone who was supposed to support and be of encouragement to me and not look down on my "fault" was very disturbing. I must admit that along with some other things, pushed me away from the church. So I can say that I understand when younger persons are not interested in going to church. We do not want to be reminded of things that should not be done every single church service, but instead inspire us to grow spiritually and to help enlighten our spirit and faith in God.

After finding out I was pregnant, I made this promise to God that if he would be my Alpha and Omega (my beginning and end) during this time, I would draw closer to HIM and live the life that he has for me so that my son could see me as an example of Christ.

Two and a half years ago, I found a church home that was for me. I have been able to develop lifelong friendships and relationships with others in the church that have the same goals as me that keep me pressing on daily. I have been able to grow in all aspects of my life including spiritually, mentally, physically, intellectually, and emotionally. This is needed in my life and I am thankful for those who have become a part of it.

CHAPTER FIVE: TODDLERS' VIEW

It's all about me mommy!!!

It's 7:40 a.m. and I'm running late (as usual) because I have to take Cayden to school and be to work at 8:00 a.m. It's one of those mornings where he is in his cranky mood.

Me: "Ok Cayden time to go! Turn off that DVD player."

Cayden: "No! I wanna watch my DVD player."

Me: "It's time to go and I'm leaving. Bye!"

He starts crying and clings to me to pick him up.

"Cayden, mommy has her purse, book bag and your bag so my hands are already full. I don't have eight arms to carry you and everything else."

After several minutes of him standing there crying and me being frustrated because I'm behind schedule, I manage to carry him and everything else out the house and to the car. A typical toddler's thought process "Mommy is superwoman".

That may be funny but it is true. I tried to finish all my schoolwork and other obligations I had before I came to the house because as soon as I walked in, it was "MOMMY, MOMMY!!" and all my focus went to him. He then proceeds to tell me about his day and whatever else that he is so anxious to share with me. To see him smile and hear him talk about his day, even though that sometimes I can't understand, is the highlight of my day.

Now there are days where I'm like "ok really Cayden….how do you know so much". Or why did I wish you could start talking again (because now he won't stop). But the conversations are priceless. The car rides are the best. Most of the time it's not even real conversations between him and me but more like one-sided thoughts that he has and if I contest his thoughts then I'm wrong. So all my answers usually consists of a few words like "wow", "uh huh", "they did?" (unsure of who "they" are), and "Yes you are a big boy".

This is his typical one-sided conversation car ride where ever we were going:

The younger Cayden:

Cayden: "Mommy…what is my name?

It seems my answer that comes seconds later is too long for him and he answers his own question: Cayden Tristan Dillard" …I know how to spell it too" (and he spells it)

"Mommy, why are you going through the yellow light? Green means GO; yellow means SLOW DOWN, red means STOP"

"Mommy, can I play a game on your phone? I know how to get to it. I'm a big boy"

The older Cayden:

Me: "Ok Cayden, we are almost to your school it's time to put the game away". He looks up from his game and takes a look to see if we are really at the school and says, "No mommy you didn't pull in yet, I still have a few more minutes".

"Mommy, are you being a team player right now? I don't think you are". This line may come if I say he can't go to the park or do something.

And I can't help but to laugh to myself because he really is such a smart guy.

And it goes on and on and on until we reach our destination. But I wouldn't pass these seemingly minor things up. These are our bonding moments. Although I may not answer him, I am listening to him because it amazes me how much he knows and how he can form sentences so well. No, I couldn't have given him up. Where would I be without him?

At times I did feel sad because I wasn't able to be there with him in the evenings because I was either working or at school. My mom kept him during this time. This eased my mind because I did not have to worry about him while I was trying to focus on school. I had to keep telling myself that this will all pay off soon. Others told me I need to complete my education while he is still young because he won't remember much. If anything he can say "my mom worked really hard while I was little to provide a great life for us".

A most recent thing that he said to me was when I took him to Chucke Cheese and McDonald's on a Saturday. He told me "Mommy, you make my heart happy". I just smiled and thanked God for him because if no one else loves me, my little man will. These are the moments that I will cherish forever.

CHAPTER SIX: MAKING TIME

Finding an outlet to keep your sanity

Recently, I was involved in a community program through the Chamber of Commerce called Strive2Thrive. This is a program that empowers families living in poverty. The dictionary defines poverty as: "the state or condition of having little or no money, goods, or means of support; condition of being poor." So, I use the word poverty to mean not living on the streets or in a shelter, but poverty meaning families who are working a regular 9am-5pm job but still barely making it from one paycheck to another. With the economy today, that includes most of the middle class families. Strive2Thrive teaches families how to change the mindset and to not think like this is how it has to be. Classes include: self-development, leadership and development skills, managing finances, healthy cooking, resume writing, job interviewing and more. The program also helps with resources to enable those who could not obtain their high school diploma to take classes so that they can get their GED. Being in this program was like an outlet for me to keep sane and to know that I was not the only one in this situation. It also enabled me to meet new families of all different backgrounds and to share some of their experiences and one common goal: Receiving a hand up and not a hand out. On July 25, 2013, I along with 6 other families completed the 2 1/2 year program and we are now on our way to being more self-sufficient.

Because I always had this need for more and still not financially stable enough to move back to Kennesaw, I enrolled into Albany State University (ASU) in the fall 2011. In the summer of 2012, I was accepted into a research program Minority Biomedical Research Support-Research Initiative for Scientific Enhancement program (MBRS-RISE). The goals of this program are to increase the skills and interest of students and faculty in biomedical research, develop on-campus research programs and increase the number of under-represented minorities engaged in biomedical research. Being in this program enabled me to better my laboratory technique skills and gain valuable insight in the various fields of research. I was also able to interact with other students who had the same career interests and goals as me. I connected with mentors of the program and was given advice and guidance as far as what direction to take after I graduated. I had connected with an awesome mentor at ASU that has allowed me to work in his lab. My research project involved seeing the effects of an antioxidant (Curcumin) on a heterocyclic amine (MeIQ) that has the potential to cause cancer when meats (chicken, beef, or pork) are cooked at high temperatures and for long periods of time.

Performing research allowed me to do what I loved the most: helping others. My first career choice when I first graduated high school was nursing. I just knew I was going to be a nurse because I loved helping people and putting their needs before mine. I have this huge heart and I care a lot about people. But as I was exposed to other career options, research sparked my interest. I could still do what I was passionate about but in a different manner. With research it takes my mind off of my personal life and allows me to find solutions that could eventually help others locally, nationally, and even globally.

Although my life was already jam packed, I found that I could fit one more extracurricular organization into and that was Florida-Georgia Louis Stokes Alliance for Minority Participation (FGLSAMP). This program is a National Science Foundation (NSF) Project, which includes over 1000 talented undergraduates in Science, Technology,

Engineering, and Mathematics (STEM) majors. It is a coalition of twelve institutions in Florida and one in Georgia. The primary focus of FGLSAMP is to increase the number of baccalaureate degrees granted to underrepresented students in the STEM disciplines. This is another form of networking with students of various disciplines. The program also allowed for travel to different schools of interest so that I could gain valuable information needed to further my career.

Being involved in such programs at ASU granted me opportunities that I may not have gotten elsewhere. In November 2012, I along with twelve other Albany State University students travelled to San Jose, California to attend a major research conference the Annual Biomedical Research

Conference for Minority Students (ABRCMS). There were over 2000 students and over 500 universities and colleges from across the nation. This was such an awesome experience. I also attended two other research conferences at Morehouse School of Medicine and at Emory University. I acquired great insight in various fields and different subjects and planned on carrying these experiences with me as I continued my educational journey.

CHAPTER SEVEN: CLIMBING OVER THE MOUNTAIN

Will I ever reach the top?

There were (and still are) days when I just wanted to jump inside of a well and never come out. It literately gets that tough, but I know that I cannot give up. I have come too far. I am reminded every day of the little person that God has blessed me with and I know that there is always sunshine after the rain. As stated before, I had enrolled into ASU in 2011. On May 4, 2013, through all the trials and tribulations (and being told it was going to take me longer than 2 years to complete this degree), I proudly walked across the stage and was awarded the degree of Bachelors of Science in Biology with a concentration in Biotechnology. Education is a very important factor in my life and because I want to have some influence in the minority and under-represented communities, I must still go farther. By August 2014, I intend on enrolling into graduate school to complete my Master's of Public Health with an emphasis on Epidemiology, and then continuing on to obtain my PhD in Behavioral Health/Sciences. I want to make a positive difference in the healthcare and clinical research communities and to have an impact on policy decisions at the state and federal level through my work. Epidemiology is the cornerstone of Public Health because this is how scientists, researchers, biologists, and others discover how disease patterns develop as well as the causes and effects on health conditions in populations. As a young, African American female, I have a passion to help those who are members of under-represented groups, specifically by informing them about issues regarding their health and improving health disparities. This is my most precious and ultimate goal. Combining what I have learned in these short years of being a mother, along with my faith and trust in God, my family and community activities, I know I will see the peak of this mountain.

This journey has not been easy and I have experienced hardships as I still experience them today. I stated earlier in Chapter 2 that I would explain more about "the system". This in particular is the government; or should I say the programs that the government has implemented into society that have policies in which they don't seem to actually help those people who are trying to make a better life for themselves. I personally have experienced this:

Department of Family and Children Services (Foodstamps)

I had gone to the local DFCS office to apply for food stamps after returning home. I was immediately approved for approximately $330. Now that was a lot because it was only me and my unborn child. But I utilized them as my appetite was heavier then. In order to continue receiving benefits, every six months or so there is a review. This is to report any changes in income or jobs that may have come during this time. When my review had come around,

I had given birth to Cayden and I was working and I had applied for child support. Because the policy is to report all forms of income whether it is earned (job) or unearned (Social Security, Child Support, Disability, etc.), I had to report all my earnings. I then went from receiving over $300 to about $250 in food stamps. That was still plenty for me and my child.

Moving forward to most recently, I now have my own car and have a better paying job, so therefore I have been cut all the way down to $60 in food stamps! The system does not look at the fact that I am still a single mother, working only 14 hours at the pharmacy, and was a full time student. It sees this: I don't have multiple children, am not receiving

TANF (Temporary Assistance for Needy Families), has a decent place of living, has a car and is working on higher education; therefore I'm doing great and don't need any assistance. Despite furthering my education, working at the pharmacy, and taking advantage of various opportunities that are presented to me, I still have my daily struggles and still need a little help.

Department of Family and Children Services (Childcare)

I had a review to come up for my childcare services. I sent all my paperwork in on time. I received a letter a few weeks later stating that I could no longer receive services because I stopped working for a certain period of time. The letter also stated I owed $500. Of course that wasn't right. I actually had two jobs at the time (restaurant and had gotten a part-time position at ATC), and was still attending school. I appealed this decision but because I couldn't contact the person I needed to talk with, my childcare services were cut completely. That had me down for just a moment as I had to pick up extra shifts at work just to pay his daycare and on top of that my car note. But I was still determined to keep pressing.

Albany Technical College

In my continuing education, I had some setbacks. I was in the Pharmacy Technology program and the time had come to start my internship. I was excited. This meant that I was almost done. I received a phone call a couple weeks before intern and it was my professor to say that the quarter I sat out due to personal reasons, they added a health class that was mandatory for students to take. My professor tried to fight for me to go ahead and start my intern and just take the course along with the internship but the dean said no. I cried. I had come so far and now I had to take an extra semester because of one class. After the tears fell, I had no choice but to take the class and complete my degree.

Albany State University

The road to earning my Bachelor's degree was not an easy one. I found out that I had taken 2 classes that I didn't need! I also had to retake a class that I had completed at Darton College and passed but it wouldn't transfer due to institutional reasons. I fought hard for this class but to no avail. So, my last semester I was left with all science classes (Organic Chemistry 2, Cellular Molecular Biology, Genetic Engineering and 2 others) and they were hard! I may have come out of the semester with A's and B's and a 3.5 GPA, but I struggled throughout the semester. During midterms, my grades were consisted of a couple D's and F's (which I was not proud of), I shed many tears, and I also stated I was not finishing, that I wanted to quit. But of course I couldn't. I am living out my purpose not for myself but for my son, my family, and the many unknown people in this world that I have been placed on this earth to help. With the encouragement of the many supporters in my life, I will not give up.

Don't quit

When things go wrong, as they sometimes will,
When the road you're trudging seems all uphill,
When the funds are low and the debts are high,
And you want to smile, but you have to sigh,
When care is pressing you down a bit,
Rest, if you must, but don't you quit.
Life is queer with its twists and turns,
As every one of us sometimes learns,
And many a failure turns about,
When he might have won had he stuck it out;
Don't give up though the pace seems slow--
You may succeed with another blow.
Often the goal is nearer than,
It seems to a faint and faltering man,
Often the struggler has given up,
When he might have captured the victor's cup,
And he learned too late when the night slipped down,
How close he was to the golden crown.
Success is failure turned inside out--
The silver tint of the clouds of doubt,
And you never can tell how close you are,
It may be near when it seems so far,
So stick to the fight when you're hardest hit--
It's when things seem worst that you must not quit.
- Author unknown

ACKNOWLEDGMENTS

I would first and foremost like to give God thanks for his continuous blessings on my life. I will continue to walk in his presence and live out the purpose he has for my life.

A never ending thanks to my mother. You have been here for me since the beginning. I know at times you want to tell me "I told you so" but just know I have learned and still learning so much from you. Thank you for being the strong woman you are today.

A special shout out to my FAMILY. I thank you all for the support and encouragement. I would not be this far in my life if it wasn't for you all!

Special thanks Femi Anderson for the design of the book, Linda Brown for help with editing my book, and Jocelyn Vaughn for the design of my brand and advertising under extreme short notice! THANK YOU!

Thanks to Ausha Jackson, the director of the Strive2Thrive Program. I am honored to have been a part of such an awesome program. I have learned so much and I will apply it as I continue this journey through life.

I am also grateful for the allies in the program I have been paired with, Glenn and Dawn Clack. You all are life savers!!! ☺

Special thanks to Vincent Alston. When I first met you at Strive2Thrive, you saw something in me that I didn't. I appreciate the advice and determination that you continuously give to me.

To those dear to my heart (you know who you are), thanks for keeping me in line and helping me stay focused!!!

And to everyone I have not mentioned THANK YOU!!!

REFERENCES

http://dictionary.reference.com/browse/poverty

http://wic.ga.gov/

http://www.thedontquitpoem.com/thePoem.htm

Postpartum Depression.

http://www.ncbi.nlm.nih.gov/pubmedhealth/PMH0004481/

http://dfcs.dhs.georgia.gov/fact-sheets

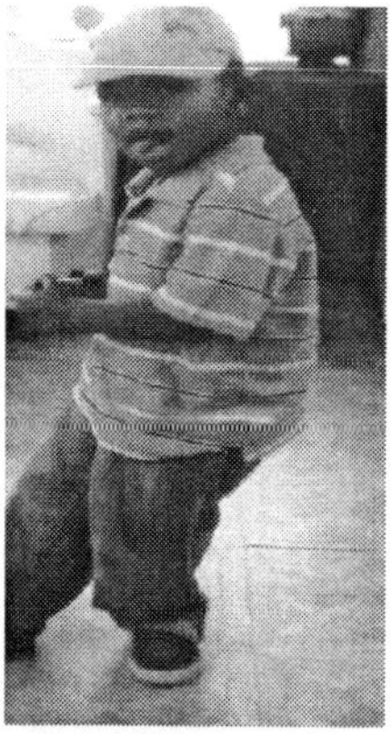
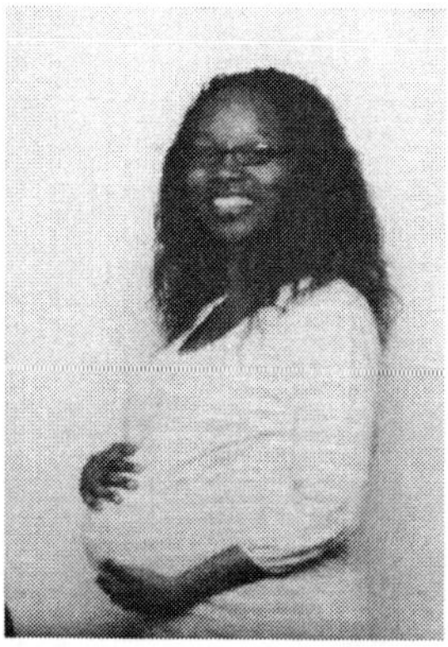
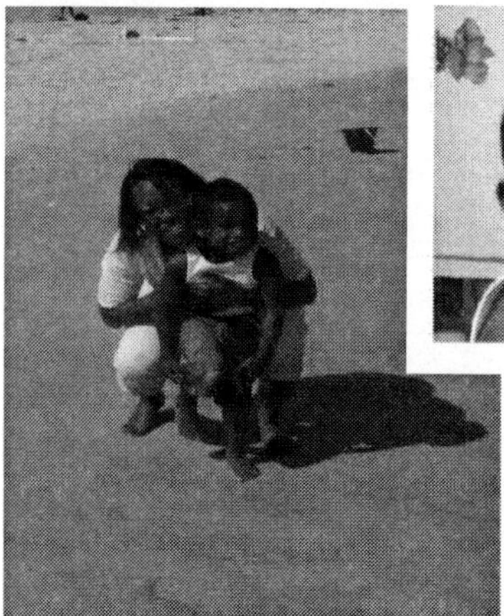
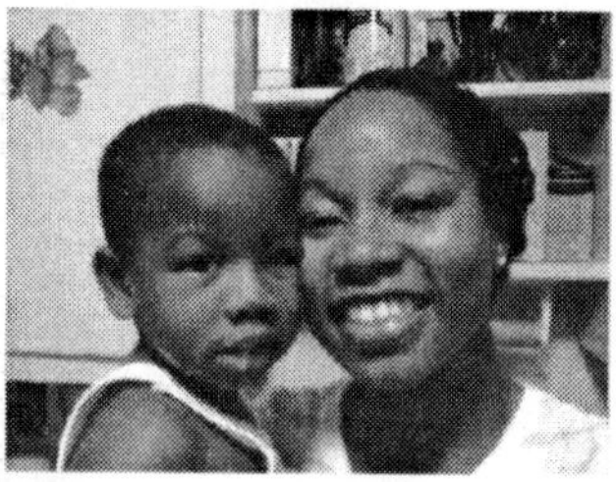
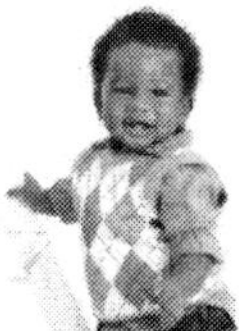